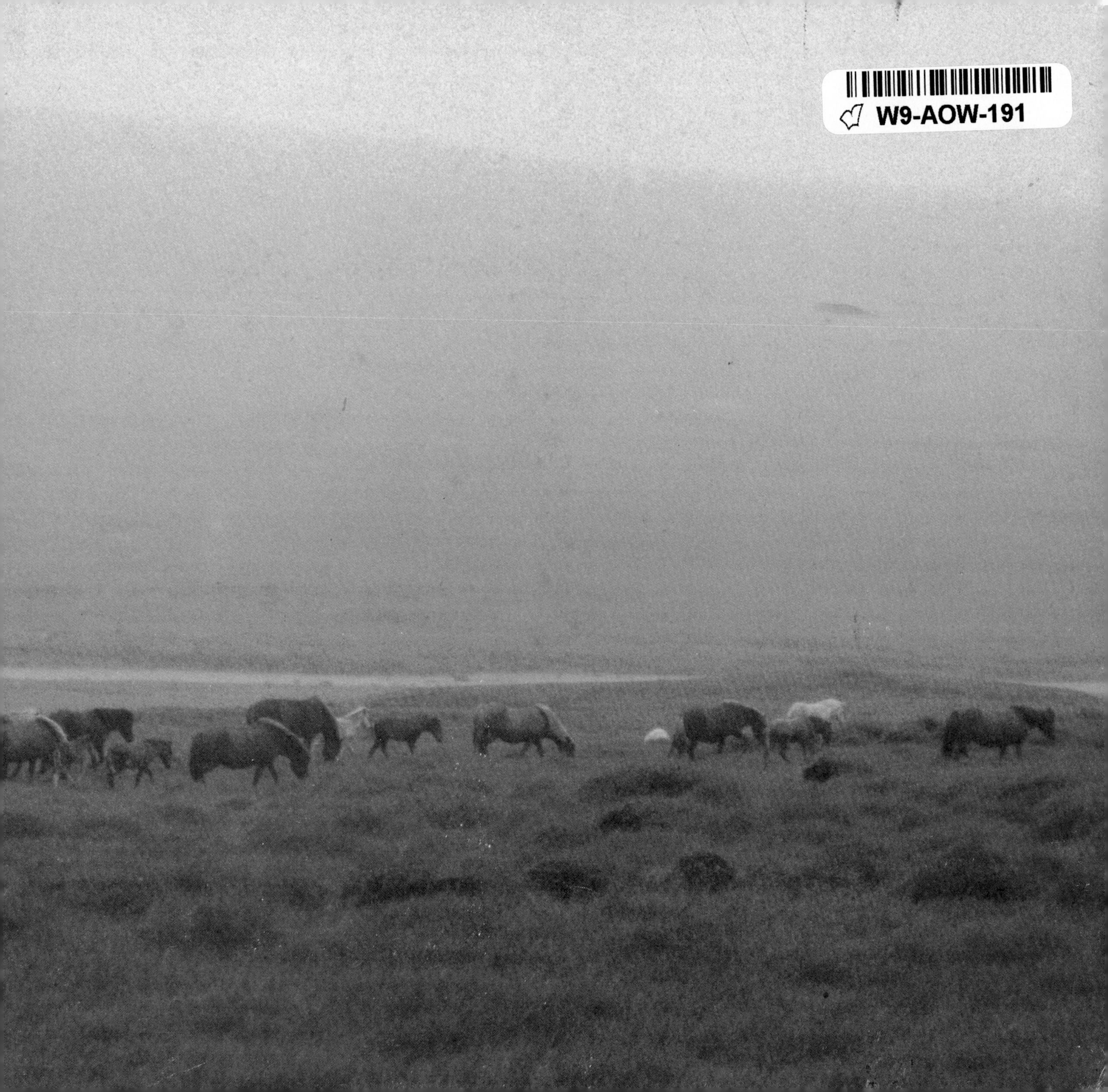

A Michael Neugebauer Book
Copyright © 1989, Neugebauer Press, Salzburg, Austria.
Published and distributed in USA by Picture Book Studio, Saxonville, MA.
Distributed in Canada by Vanwell Publishing, St.Catharines, Ont.
Published in UK by Picture Book Studio, Neugebauer Press Ltd., London.
Distributed in UK by Ragged Bears, Andover.
Distributed in Australia by Era Publications, Adelaide.
All rights reserved.
Printed in Belgium by Proost

LIBRARY OF CONGRESS CATALOGING IN PUBLICATION DATA
Kalas, Sybille
The wild horse family book/text and photographs by Sybille Kalas.
Originally published in German.
Summary: Describes, in text and photographs, the physical characteristics,
habits, and natural environment of the wild horses of Iceland.
ISBN 0-88708-110-X
1. Iceland pony – Juvenile literature. 2. Wild horses – Iceland – Juvenile literature.
[Iceland pony. 2. Wild horses. 3. Ponies.] I. Title.
SF315.2.I3K35   1989
636.1′6 – dc20   89-3929

Ask your bookseller for these other PICTURE BOOK STUDIO Animal Family Books:
THE CHIMPANZEE FAMILY BOOK by Jane Goodall
THE GOOSE FAMILY BOOK by Sybille Kalas
THE BEAVER FAMILY BOOK by Sybille and Klaus Kalas
THE PENGUIN FAMILY BOOK by Lauritz Sømme and Sybille Kalas
THE LION FAMILY BOOK by Angelika Hofer and Günter Ziesler

Sybille Kalas **The Wild Horse Family Book**

Translated by Patricia Crampton

PICTURE BOOK STUDIO

Annkatrin feels at home with horses. She likes to be in the midst of the herd as the horses trot along, their manes floating freely. These Icelandic ponies still live together in exactly the same way as their ancestors, the wild horses.

Annkatrin's dream is to live like that, wild and free with a roaming herd.

Among the many races or breeds of horses, there are some which are still so like their wild ancestors that they can live a free, independent life in natural surroundings.

One such race is the Icelandic pony, small and sturdy, tough and resistant, lively, alert and not easily excited. They are well-suited to a free life under hard environmental conditions in Iceland, their native island in the North Atlantic.

Here is Annkatrin with Skjoni, an Icelandic skewbald pony.

Annkatrin knows them all by name: Vindur and Nasi, Starni, Haeringur, Funi, and Lýsingur. The ancestors of these ponies arrived here 1100 years ago, on Viking ships, with the first settlers from Norway.

Since then, men and ponies have helped one another to live in their island home. Even now it is natural for most people in Iceland to have ponies – several of them, not just one, though even that is quite unusual in most countries.
The herds of Icelandic ponies spend the entire summer roaming freely across the broad, almost unpopulated Icelandic countryside. This is the place where Annkatrin's dream of living among the horses can come true.

When you hear the word Iceland, you probably think of an island of volcanic eruptions, hot springs and geysers. But even without these, Iceland is unusual, because the natural world surrounds you wherever you go.

All our senses respond to the silent valley, encircled by cloud-veiled mountains, to the spray of a waterfall, to the beach of fine, black sand, where you stand alone, except for the seabirds. And over there, on the far side of the mountain meadows, the dome of a glacier stands out like a huge, shimmering shell on the horizon.

Many of the herds spend the summer far from the inhabited areas, criss-crossing the vast mountain pastures. These shy, independent ponies are not easy to track down and watch.

But other herds stay close to the farms even in summertime. Their summer pastures are the green hilly slopes, with their clear streams, where the salmon leap.

Between stony hillsides, on which lichens and dwarf birches grow, lie marshy stretches of meadow dotted with small lakes.
These ponies are used to people and neither avoid us nor run away,
as the herds on the high ground would, but greet us with lively curiosity.
Perhaps they will even allow us to share in their lives for a little while.

Even at a distance we recognize the black stallion, the only full-grown male in the herd, by the way he behaves. The sight of us has aroused his attention and curiosity, but he is also ready to warn or even to defend the mares, foals and yearlings, his wives and children. If he feels any alarm, a single warning snort will be enough to send the whole herd thundering away in wild flight.

So we approach the ponies slowly, not walking straight towards them, but moving as if we too were animals, grazing comfortably. We talk quietly to them and wait for them to come to us of their own accord.

The first to come to us is always a mare, while the stallion still looks on distrustfully from a distance.

Now we are in the midst of the herd, which is home to the young foals. Here they feel safe and protected, no matter how far they wander, whether by the sea or in river valleys, or on hills, mountains, or upland meadows.

The herd gives the foals everything they need.
Their mothers, above all, provide not only the milk which makes them strong and healthy, but also the care, tender affection, and protection which they need while they are still young.

As the foals gain experience in the herd, they grow into the self-assured, well-balanced animals so much valued by the Icelanders as reliable saddle ponies and often their sole companions in their island wilderness. This skewbald pony is already two years old, but he is still drinking his mother's milk. This is only possible because she has not had another foal meanwhile.

The security their mothers give them make the foals feel safe enough to go adventuring. They soon make friends with other foals, first sniffing cautiously at one another, then running races, playing follow-the-leader, stooping and lashing out with their hooves.

This young female pony wants to know more about us. Step by step she moves closer, her velvet nostrils twitching as she tests the strange smell. The alert, long-lashed dark eyes are quite close to us now, the ears pricked inquisitively forward. But then the pony thinks better of it, lifts her head and gives a high whinny.

Her mother answers immediately and she turns and gallops back on her long, gawky legs. The foal must certainly have known all the time where the mare was grazing and waiting for her.

Protected by their mothers, the foals gradually become familiar with the herd and the hilly surroundings, trotting easily over the thousands of hillocks on the Icelandic meadows. Neither Annkatrin herself, nor a horse from another country could do as well. But Iceland's children can run across the hummocky meadows as naturally as the Icelandic ponies.

You have probably noticed how lumpy and knobbly the meadows are. The bumps and furrows are caused by the frequent alternation of frost and warmth, the freezing and thawing of the upper layer of earth. Under the spring sun the soil thaws faster in some places and slower in others, according to the length of time the sun shines on them, how wet they are, and what plants grow on them. This causes tensions in the earth which make it bulge into hummocks.

Iceland may sound cold and uncomfortable, but when the midday sun shines on the many hummocks and warms the soft cushions of moss and lichen, a bumpy meadow makes a comfortable bed for young ponies. Mother and child are quite relaxed, looking as if nothing could disturb them, but they can be wide awake and ready for flight if need be.

Our herd is moving on now, led by a mare, with the stallion at the rear, making sure that everyone is coming. All the young ponies – large and small – walk close behind their mothers.

The ponies may be moving towards water, or to one of the good grazing grounds, perhaps in a sheltered spot, or on some dry, sandy hill where it is fun to roll. Gradually we learn all the places our ponies like best so we can take our time and look around while we follow them, safe in the knowledge that we will soon find them again.

In the marshland between reeds and cotton grass lies a little secret pool, which reflects the clouds as if in a dark eye. It is quiet here − so quiet, you can feel it. Only the piping calls of the golden plover can be heard, but far from disturbing the quiet, they make it still deeper, wider and more infinite.

Dwarf birches, crowberries and gentians grow on a dry hillside on the edge of the marsh. Stones, moss and lichen are warmed by the sun, and you can smell the scent of thyme when you crouch down to gather the black crowberries, which taste both sweet and bitter and satisfy your thirst and hunger.

We have found the plovers' nest, but we walk on quickly, because we do not want to frighten them.

At their resting-place, sheltered from the wind by a hill, the ponies are dozing with half-shut eyes. Only the black mare lifts her head and sniffs the air in our direction.

The half-grown skewbald pony – the one still taking milk from his mother – is the first to come to us and sniff curiously at Annkatrin. She once brought him a piece of bread and since then he has been quite bold and inquisitive. Annkatrin is delighted, and gives him more bread, but when the skewbald's curiosity turns to the stallion and he tries to challenge him, the results are different. The stallion will not stand for that kind of thing.

He immediately teaches the skewbald who is boss, but this is not a real fight, just a playful scrap between the two males.

You can see from every movement they make, from the way they hold themselves and the expressions on their faces, that the black horse is the superior, the more assured and proud full-grown male, who finally drives the young scamp back to his mother.

Although it was not a serious clash, the stallion now marks out his herd's territory with urine, scrapes with his hoof and sniffs at his scent marks, still watched curiously by the impudent youngster.

Then the stallion fleers – lifting his head and drawing back his lips, he absorbs the scent of his mares, his wives, many already bearing his foals, which will be born next spring.

Peace returns to the herd. Many of the mares stay close together in pairs, tending each other's coats. If they nibbled at you like that with their big horses' teeth, you would be badly bruised.

But if feels good to the ponies, who may stand together for a long time, busily nibbling at the roots of each other's tails and at necks and manes. This helps to keep their summer coats smooth and gleaming, but the mutual grooming also makes for a friendly and relaxed atmosphere within the herd.

Friendly and relaxed – that is how we feel, too, when we join the Icelandic ponies on their summer pastures. Lie down on the grass, close your eyes and listen to the muffled tread of hooves on the mossy ground as the ponies move slowly across it, grazing. Listen to the steady tearing and crunching of grass and the occasional soft whinny from one of the ponies.

Now, in the late afternoon sunshine, each pony seeks out his preferred spot, beside his mother, safe and close to the source of milk…

...or alone and apart on the hillside, gazing into the broad, blue yonder.

The Icelandic summer day is by no means over yet. Dusk comes late in the evening, but this is a good time for a little rest. With a soft hummock of meadow for a pillow, among dwarf birches and sun-warmed cushions of moss, pony child and human child fall asleep, probably dreaming the same dreams…

...dreams of green hills and quiet lakes, of wandering through moors and valleys, across rivers and mountains – of bird songs and cloudy skies – of a pony blowing down his nostrils in the stillness...
Annkatrin will go on dreaming of her first summer with the Icelandic ponies for a very long time.